THE BREAD MACHINE

COOKBOOK

The Right Recipes for Perfect Bakery Bread, Buns, and Sweets. As Delicious as The Artisanal Ones. Whether You're a Beginner or Expert, This is The Right Cookbook for You

JESSICA **FRALEY**

Table of Contents

INTRODUCTION

Bread is a baked meal made from various forms of dough that can be cooked. Normally, the dough is composed of flour and water. In hundreds of ways, shapes, sorts, and textures, bread is baked. Flour and other ingredients differ in quantities and forms, as do preparation methods. Bread has been one of the most important foods in history since it is still one of the oldest artificial foods. In fact, since the dawn of agriculture, people have been making bread.

For every meal of the day, people of different communities serve bread in diverse ways. As part of the dinner or as a single snack, it may be consumed.

The best thing is freshly baked bread! The only trouble is time and commitment are required. Many people have never dreamed of making fresh bread in their lives, but much of that has begun to change with the new advent of automated bread-making machines. Today, millions of people turn their kitchens into bakeries, and every day they enjoy their own freshly made bread at a fraction of the price they might spend in a shop.

Like someone who makes his bread, it's a much better choice to make bread at home than buying bread at a bakery or even some bakeries, where most bread is made with some degree of change in baking. You can select healthier ingredients when choosing which ingredients to use in your food, whether it's whole wheat, organic flour, gluten-free bread, or any other food restrictions or preferences

Chapter 1: Let's Learn About Bread Machine

A kitchen appliance for baking bread is called a bread machine. A bread machine contains a tin or bread pan that has built-in paddles. They are placed in the middle of a small oven.

1.1 How does a bread machine function?

You will place kneading paddles in the pan first. You will measure the ingredients as the tin comes out from the machine and load the ingredients into the tin.

Afterward, you only need to position the pan inside the oven (machine), select the settings of the bread machine in the electronic panel, and close the door. Here, the magic bread maker takes over!

Kneading the dough is one of the first things the bread machine can do. You can hear the sounds. If your bread maker comes with a display window, you can watch the whole baking process, which is very intriguing.

All will go quiet for some time after the kneading process is finished, and after it, the growing phase starts. The bread machine helps the dough to rest and rise. Then, there will be another kneading round and the rising process.

Finally, it will turn on the bread maker's oven, and you will feel the steam rising from the steam vent.

1.2 What kinds of bread machines are there?

Most of the devices that produce bread would be a little bit different. This is due to the reason that a bread maker is built to fulfill a specific role in each variety. The most popular varieties of bread makers available on the modern market are:

Vertical

As the bread tin is formed in this direction, most of the bread machines bake loaves, which are placed vertically. There is only one kneading paddle for this sort of bread machine.

Horizontal

These types of bread makers contain two kneading paddles in their pan. These bread machines can bake horizontal-shaped bread-like similar to the one available at superstores.

Small

For minimal kitchen space or if you don't eat a lot of bread, small bread machines are perfect. These little kitchen helpers do not take up most of the counter space and provide a couple or one person with enough bread.

Large

In large families, large bread machines come in handy; when you have a lot of people at the table, the bread will vanish very easily. The large bread makers that produce 3 lb. of bread loaves can serve a large family.

Gluten-Free

Many machines are built to satisfy the needs of healthy-eating people with the great abundance of bread-making styles on the market.

1.3 How to use a bread machine?

The baking method is quite the same everywhere, regardless of which bread machine you select. You add the ingredients into the tin, then put the bread pan in the machine and select the settings you want.

Depending on the model of the machine, the usual method of baking takes somewhere between 2 to 5 hours. It is best to place a loaf on a wire rack at the end of the baking period to cool off before eating it.

These four ingredients are a must while baking bread.

- Flour

- Yeast

- Liquid(water, milk, or any other)

- Salt

You can add any other extras that you want, including raisins, almonds, chocolate chips, and the like, in addition to the main ingredients.

While the method of bread baking can seem very basic and basic, some tips will make you a bread baking pro with a bread machine:

Check and observe the handbook/instructions. The dry ingredients should be incorporated first for some bread makers while the wet ingredients go in first for others.

Besides, please remember that not all bread makers are made equal when reading baking bread recipes. Some produce 1 pound lb. others make 1.5 and 2 pound lb. There are some versions of the bread machine which are capable to bake 3lb. loaves.

It is important to match the quantities of ingredients to the recipes usually used in the bread machine when testing out a new recipe. It is really necessary not to surpass the bread machine pan's capacity.

If the recipe has milk in it then the use of a delayed mixing period is not advised.

1.4 What kinds of bread can you make with a bread machine?

There are many different programs for producing many different styles of the loaf for most bread makers. By using various types of flour and varying the other ingredients, you can produce whole wheat, white bread, or special loaves. On its display screen, you can see the different choices the bread maker provides (from the top: basic, whole wheat, multigrain, French, pizza, and bake only). You simply bring a slightly different mix into the pan at the beginning for different slices of bread and choose a different program from the show, and the bread maker can automatically manage various kneading, rising, and baking periods, and so on. (So French loaves get a longer rising time, whole wheat loaves require more preheating, sweetbreads require longer kneading and rising times, and dark-colored crusty bread requires extra baking time.) Some bread makers even offer a fast-baking mode through which the bread loaf gets ready in almost halftime but the performance will be slightly less refined. Not quite such an impressive raise or even blend. Baking bread takes time and persistence, and if you hurry it, you can't expect flawless results.

1.5 What else can you make in a bread machine?

The best thing these days about most bread makers is that you can cook all sorts of stuff in them. In a bread machine, except for the bread, you can make something like pizza dough and rolls also. In a bread machine, you can also make brownies, biscuits, and cake conveniently.

Most machines have a Jam function built-in. You can make tasty jams and jellies in your bread machine. You may also use this setting for producing syrups and puddings as well. Scrambled eggs are a simple meal that whips together in no time if your bread maker has the blade near to its bottom.

So, the options are endless. You just have to be creative.

1.6 Benefits of a bread machine

You can enjoy the fresh-baked homemade bread, first of all. Many bread machines often have a timer feature that allows the baking period to be set at a certain time. This functionality is really helpful anytime you want to get hot bread for breakfast in the morning.

You're able to control what you eat. You can easily regulate what components come into the loaf by baking bread at home. This choice is convenient for those with allergies or for others who try to control the consumption of any of the ingredients.

It's an easy job to make bread in a bread maker. Some people think making bread baking at home is a tough process but with a bread machine baking bread is fun. You

just select the desired option and relax - within the bread maker, all the combining, growing, and baking operation is taking place, which also makes it a zero mess process.

In the long run, it saves you lots of money. If you think it is inexpensive to buy bread at a supermarket, you may be mistaken. Baking bread at home will save you money in the long term, especially if you have any dietary restrictions.

Different kinds of bread can be created by bread machines: gluten-free bread, rye bread, whole wheat bread, and hundreds of other forms. Pasta dough, jam, pizza dough, and a variety of other tasty recipes can be made as well.

1.7 Is a Bread machine worth it?

If you need to make a lot of loaves or need extra comfort, you can get a bread machine. You may be tired of hand-making bread and have a busy life, so this machine is a solution to these problems. Bread machines are very easy, useful, and worth any penny at the end of the day.

Bread machines cost from 65 USD up to 320 USD everywhere. How much bread you're going to make will decide how long it will be before the bread machine expenses are covered and you start saving your money. If you are a huge family that enjoys a lot of bread regularly, there is no question that baking bread at home is the most economical alternative.

For a very long time, bread machines (not inexpensive ones) would last. Some people are using the same bread machines for more than 10 years.

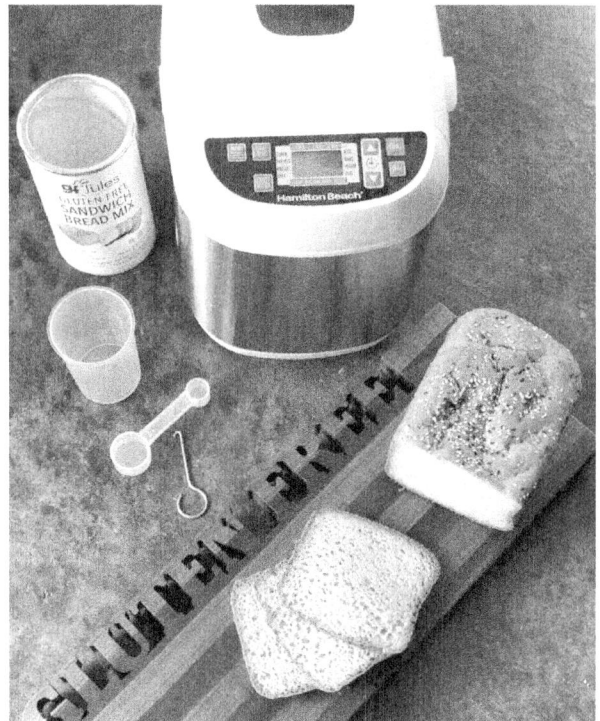

Chapter 2: Basic Bread recipes

2.1 Bread machine Naan

Total time

2 hours 25 minutes

Servings

6 servings

Nutrition facts

363 calories per serving

Ingredients

Here is the list of ingredients required to make these bread machine naans.

- 4 cups bread flour

- 1 large egg at room temperature (beaten)

- 2 tbsp. canola oil

- ¾ cup warm milk

- 2 tsp. sugar

- ¾ cup plain yogurt

- 2 tsp. active dry yeast

- 1 tsp. salt

- 1 tsp. baking powder

Method

Follow the instructions below to prepare these flavorful bread naans.

1. Place all ingredients in the bread machine pan in the order recommended by the maker. Select the dough cycle. After mixing for 5 minutes, check the dough and add 1 to 2 tbsp. of water if required.

2. Place the dough onto a lightly floured surface when the cycle is finished. Divide your dough into six parts and shape them into balls. Roll every ball into a ¼ inches thick oval. Leave it for 5 minutes to rest.

3. Brush the top of naan with water and place it in a greased large skillet with a wet side down. Cover and cook it for 1 minute over medium to high heat. Turn the position of naan over and cook the other side for about 30 seconds or until done.

4. Repeat these steps for all the naans.

5. Enjoy them with your favorite curry.

2.2 Whole wheat cornmeal bread

Total time

2 hours 10 minutes

Servings

12 servings

Nutrition facts

150 calories per serving

Ingredients

Here is the list of ingredients required to make wheat cornmeal bread.

- 2 ¾ cups bread **flour**

- ¾ cup **cornmeal**

- ¾ cup whole wheat flour

- 2 tbsp. unsalted butter (softened)

- 1 ½ cups water at room temperature

- 1 ½ tsp. salt

- 2 ½ tsp. instant **yeast**

- 2 tbsp. brown sugar

- 1 large egg (beaten)

Method

Follow the instructions below to prepare whole wheat cornmeal bread.

1. Collect all the ingredients.

2. Add the above ingredients into the bread machine pan in the order recommended by the bread machine manufacturer.

3. Select the basic cycle and choose medium crust in settings.

4. Remove the dough from the pan when formed.

5. Transfer the dough into a 9*5* inches loaf pan.

6. Rest the dough for about 45 minutes or until it doubles.

7. The oven should be preheated to 350 °F.

8. Bake the bread in the oven for 30-40 minutes or until the bread is golden brown.

9. Serve warm and enjoy.

2.3 Seeded whole Grain loaf

Total time

4 hour 20 minutes

Servings

16 servings

Nutrition facts

128 calories per serving

Ingredients

Here is the list of ingredients required to make seeded whole grain loaf.

- 3 cups whole wheat flour
- 1 ¼ cups lukewarm milk
- 2 tbsp. canola oil
- 3 tbsp. honey
- 1 ¼ tsp. salt
- 1 tbsp. sunflower kernels
- 1 tbsp. cracked wheat
- 2 tbsp. old-fashioned oats
- 1 tbsp. millet
- 4 tsp. vital wheat gluten
- 2 ¼ tsp. active dry yeast
- 1 tbsp. flaxseed

Method

Follow the instructions below to prepare the pepperoni cheese bread.

1. In the order suggested by the manufacturer, put ingredients into the pan of a

1 1/2 to 2-pound bread machine.

2. Select the basic simple bread settings. Then press start.

3. Remove the pan from the machine once the cycle is completed.

4. Take out the bread from the pan sometimes you have to shake the bread to remove it from the pan.

5. Place it on a cooling rack.

6. Slice and enjoy.

2.4 Best Bread Machine Bread Recipe

Total time

3 hours 10 minutes

Servings

20 servings

Nutrition facts

163 calories per serving

Ingredients

Here is the list of ingredients required to make this simple bread.

- 4 cups all-purpose flour

- 2 tsp. sugar

- 2 tsp. oil

- 2 1/2 tsp active dry yeast

- 1½ cups warm water

- 2 tsp. salt

Method

Follow the instructions below to make the bread.

1. Sift the flour

2. In the pan of the bread machine, add warm water.

3. Sprinkle the active dry yeast on warm water and layer it with sugar.

4. Allow the yeast to activate.

5. After five minutes, add flour, oil, and salt to the pan.

6. Select the basic setting of the machine and press the start button.

7. Once the baking time is finished take the bread out from the pan.

8. Cool it on the cooling rack.

9. Slice and enjoy your breakfast.

2.5 Semmel Bread

Total time

1 hour 20 minutes

Servings

4 servings

Nutrition facts

450 calories per serving

Ingredients

Here is the list of ingredients required to make semmel bread.

- 2 ½ cups flour

- 2 tbsp. olive oil (extra-virgin)

- 1 tsp. sugar

- ½ cup milk

- 4 tsp. yeast

- 1 tsp. sugar

Method

Follow the instructions below to make semmel bread.

1. Dissolve the yeast with a teaspoon of sugar and warm milk.

2. In the bread machine pan, put the milk and the olive oil and add the flour and salt on top.

3. Set the kneading setting of the bread machine for approximately 1.5 hours.

4. Check the dough for the first 10 minutes (add a few tbsp. of milk, if it is too sticky. Add some flour if it is too soft) and scratch the bowl with a wooden spoon. The consistency of the prepared dough should be elastic, soft, and smooth.

5. Shape it into 5 or 6 balls once the dough is ready, each ball should weigh

approximately 150 grams. With a sharp knife, make incisions in the rolls.

6. On a floured baking sheet, place the rolls and put the sheet in a cold oven.

7. For 1 minute, turn the oven on and turn it off. For 30 minutes, leave the rolls in the oven.

8. Turn the oven on to 200 °C without opening the oven door and bake for 20 to 25 minutes. (Cover with a layer of aluminum foil or wax paper if the bread continues to brown too much.)

9. Remove the bread from the pan and let it cool on a wire rack.

2.6 Bread machine Butter bread recipe

Total time

3hours 5 minutes

Servings

12 servings

Nutrition facts

233 calories per serving

Ingredients

Here is the list of ingredients required to make bread machine butter bread.

- 1½ cups milk

- 3 cups bread flour

- 1 cup oatmeal

- 8 tbsp. butter

- 2 tbsp. sugar

- 1 ½ tbsp. bread machine yeast

- 1 tsp. salt

Method

Follow the instructions below to make butter bread.

1. Collect all the ingredients.

2. In the bread machine's pan, add the ingredients in the order specified (or suggested by the manufacturer of your bread machine). Just be careful that the yeast does not come into contact with the liquid by putting it at the top of the ingredients in a shallow well.

3. Choose a basic cycle and medium crust in the settings,

4. Start Press.

5. When the baking time is complete, remove the bread.

6. When allowed to cool first, the bread would slice best.

2.7 Fat-Free Whole Wheat Bread

Total time

2 hours 35 minutes

Servings

12 servings

Nutrition facts

134 calories per serving

Ingredients

Here is the list of ingredients required to make fat-free whole bread.

- 4 ½ cups whole wheat flour

- 1 ½ cups chickpea broth or water

- 2 tbsp. sugar

- 4 tbsp. wheat gluten

- 2 ½ tsp. instant yeast

- 1 ½ tsp. salt

Method

Follow the instructions below to make fat-free whole wheat bread.

1. Collect all the ingredients.

2. In the bread machine's pan, put the water or chickpea broth. Apply the remaining ingredients in the order specified (or suggested by the manufacturer of your bread machine). Make sure the yeast does not come into contact with the liquid by putting it at the top of the ingredients in a shallow well.

3. Choose a quick whole wheat cycle if you are using rapid rise yeast or a normal whole wheat cycle if you are using active dry yeast.

4. Start Press.

5. When the baking time completes, take it out from the oven.

6. When allowed to cool first, the bread would slice best.

2.8 Light and Fluffy Multigrain Sandwich Bread

Total time

2 hours 25 minutes

Servings

14 servings

Nutrition facts

143 calories per serving

Ingredients

Here is the list of ingredients required to make light and fluffy multigrain sandwich bread.

- 4 cups all-purpose flour

- 2 cups of boiling water

- ½ cup cereal (multi-grain)

- 2 ¼ tsp. instant yeast or active dry yeast

- 1 ½ tsp. fine salt

- 1 tbsp. olive oil or normal cooking oil

- 1 tbsp. honey or dark brown sugar

- 2 tsp. flax seeds

- 2 tsp. sesame seeds

- 2 tsp. poppy seeds

Method

Follow the instructions below to make light and fluffy multigrain bread.

1. Collect all the ingredients.

2. Add the bread flour, salt, cereal, oil, sugar, yeast, and seeds into the bread machine pan in the order recommended by the bread machine manufacturer.

3. Select the dough cycle in the settings and then start the machine.

4. Preheat your oven to 425 °F.

5. Before baking, brush the top of the loaf with water and sprinkle it with the remaining seed mixture.

6. Bake in preheated 425 °F oven until golden and crusty, Check your bread loaf after 20 minutes and use an aluminum sheet to cover it loosely if the crust

   is already browned.

2.9 50% Whole Wheat Bread

Total time

4 hours 8 minutes

Servings

20 servings

Nutrition facts

106 calories per serving

Ingredients

Here is the list of ingredients required to make 50% whole wheat bread.

- 1½ cup bread flour

- 1 ½ cup wheat flour

- 1 tbsp. honey

- ½ tbsp. brown sugar

- 1 cup lukewarm water

- 2 tbsp. butter (room temperature)

- 1 ½ tbsp. dry milk powder

- 1 tsp. active dry yeast

- 1 ½ tsp. salt

Method

Follow the instructions below to make this 50% Whole wheat bread.

1. Insert the kneading blade of the bread machine.

2. Following the recipe order, put the ingredients in the bread pan (or following the order and method stated in your Bread Maker's manual. Make a tiny indentation in the center of the flour with a knife or finger. Add yeast to the indentation and make sure that the liquid ingredients do not come into contact.

3. Place your bread pan into the machine.

4. Select the bread setting for "Whole Wheat". If available, select the color of the crust to medium and the size of the loaf (1.5LB). Push the Start button.

5. The bread will be mixed and cooked. Click the stop button when the baking period is over.

6. Remove the pan from the machine.

7. To gently remove the sides of the bread from the plate, use a non-stick spatula.

8. Turn the bread pan in an upside-down position onto a clean cooking surface or Wire Cooling Rack and shake gently until the bread falls onto the rack.

9. Cool before slicing for about 10-15 minutes.

10. Use an electric knife or a bread slicer to make perfect slices each time.

2.10 Bread Machine Bran Bread

Total time

2 hours 5 minutes

Servings

12 servings

Nutrition facts

89 calories per serving

Ingredients

Here is the list of ingredients required to make bran bread.

- 3 cups flour

- 3 tbsp. brown sugar

- 1 cup water

- 1 cup bran

- 1 ½ tbsp. dry milk powder

- 1 ½ tsp salt

- 2 ½ tsp. yeast

- 1 ½ tbsp. butter (melted)

Method

Follow the instructions below to make Bran bread.

1. Collect all the ingredients.

2. Add the above ingredients into the bread machine pan in the order recommended by the bread machine manufacturer.

3. Select the basic cycle and choose medium crust in settings.

4. The oven should be preheated to 350 °F.

5. Bake the bran bread for 30-40 minutes or until the bread is golden brown.

6. Serve warm and enjoy.

Chapter 3: Savory Bread recipes

3.1 Flavorful Herb Bread

Total time

3 hours 15 minutes

Servings

16 servings

Nutrition facts

125 calories per serving

Ingredients

Here is the list of ingredients required to make flavorful herb bread.

- 3 ½ cups bread flour

- 2 tbsps. sugar

- 1 cup warm milk

- 2 tbsp. butter (softened)

- 1 large egg at room temperature

- 2 tsp. active dry yeast

- ¼ cup dried minced onion

- 2 tbsp. dried parsley

- 1 ½ tsp. salt

- 1 tsp. dried oregano

Method

Follow the instructions below to prepare flavorful herb bread in the bread machine.

1. Collect all the ingredients.

2. Combine all the ingredients in the order recommended by the manufacturer in a bread machine pan. Select the simple setting for the bread. Choose the crust color and loaf size. Bake according to the instructions for bread machines. After mixing for 5 minutes check the dough and add 1 to 2 tbsp. of water if required.

3. When the bread is baked transfer it to a cooling rack.

4. Slice and enjoy.

3.2 Bread Machine Kalamata Olive Bread

Total time

2 hours 10 minutes

Servings

10 servings

Nutrition facts

163 calories per serving

Ingredients

Here is the list of ingredients required to make Kalamata olive bread.

- 3 cups bread flour

- 2 tbsp. olive oil

- 2 cups whole-wheat flour

- 1 cup lukewarm water

- ½ cup brine of olives

- ½ cup Kalamata olives

- 1 ½ tsp. salt

- 1 ½ tsp. dried basil

- 2 tbsp. sugar

- 2 tsp. active dry yeast

Method

Follow the instructions below to prepare Kalamata olive bread.

1. Take a 2-cup measure to add olive brine and lukewarm water to make it 1 ½ cups.

2. According to the preferred order of your manufacturer, add all ingredients into the pan of the bread machine except the olives.

3. Select your bread machine's wheat or basic setting.

4. When the machine beeps, add olives into the dough mixture.

5. When the cycle is completed and the loaf is baked, slice it and enjoy it with a side of olive oil or butter.

3.3 Bread Machine Rye Bread

Total time

3 hours 15 minutes

Servings

10 servings

Nutrition facts

163calories per serving

Ingredients

Here is the list of ingredients required to make rye bread.

- ½ + ½ cup dark rye flour

- 1 ¼ tsp. instant yeast bread machine yeast

- 2 + ¼ cups all-purpose flour

- 1 + ½ cups cool water

- 2 tsp. molasses

- 2 tsp. olive oil

- 2 tsp. caraway seeds

- 1 ½ tsp. table salt

- 1 egg

Method

Follow the instructions below to make rye bread.

1. Add all the ingredients (½ cup flour, ½ cup dark rye flour, 1 cup cool water, and 1 ¼ tsp of yeast) of sponge into the bread machine pan.

2. Select the setting of the dough cycle and allow the sponge to mix for 5 minutes. To clear the sides of the bowl from the dough, use a small spatula. Stop the machine and leave it for 10 to 12 hours.

3. After resting the sponge add the remaining ingredients except for the olive oil and start the dough cycle again. After five minutes of mixing add the olive oil.

4. Take the rye bread dough out from the machine onto a surface you have coated with water as the DOUGH cycle finishes.

5. Shape the dough with your wet hands and leave it to rest for 5 minutes.

6. Shape the dough into a wide circle with a diameter of around 9-10 inches, making sure to remove away all the air bubbles.

7. Fold the edges into the center and push to seal them. To make a compact ball, fold the dough from the middle.

8. Completely and thoroughly coat the inside of a pan with olive oil.

9. Place the dough ball in the oiled pan with a smooth side facing the oil.

10. Preheat your oven to 425 °F

11. Cover the loaf with a shower cap or tea towel. Enable it to rise until the initial size has doubled.

12. Use a silicone mat, a strip of parchment paper, or sprinkle some cornmeal or semolina to prepare the cookie sheet.

13. Remove the cover and gently remove the dough from the sides of the bowl using a small spatula.

14. On a prepared cookie sheet, turn the pan of dough upside down. The bread will gently fall on the tray from the pan showing the smooth side on top.

15. Whisk an egg to brush over the bread and sprinkle some salt on the top before baking.

16. Using a clean sharp knife or a razor blade, make three to five slashes over the top. They should be around 1/2-inch deep, at least. To make the cuts sufficiently wide, repeat the process if necessary.

17. Put the bread in a hot oven without delay, before the dough starts to spread out.

Bake the loaf for almost 30-40 minutes or till your loaf has a nice color on top.

18. Remove the loaf from the oven to a cooling rack. Cool for 1 hour after removing the loaf. This is a significant move. Slicing through the hot loaf will result in a gummy texture.

3.4 Bread Machine Crusty French bread

Total time

3hours 55 minutes

Servings

12 servings

Nutrition facts

453 calories per serving

Ingredients

Here is the list of ingredients required to make crusty French bread.

- 2 cups all-purpose flour
- 2 tbsp. powder milk
- 1 ½ cups water (room temperature)
- 2 cups bread flour
- 2 tsp. salt
- 2 tsp. sugar
- 2 tbsp. cornmeal
- 2 tsp. active dry yeast
- 1 tbsp. cold water
- 1 egg white
- 1 tbsp. oil

Method

Follow the instructions below to make the crusty French bread.

1. Collect the ingredients.

2. In the order listed, add oil, water, dry milk, bread flour, salt, all-purpose flour, sugar, and yeast to the bread machine.

3. Use your machine's French bread setting, but after the last kneading cycle, remove the dough. Punch down with your hands on the dough to let the air escape and now allow it to rise again (45 minutes to 1 hour), lightly knead, and let rise again before forming into loaves, using the dough cycle.

4. Spray a large cookie sheet or lightly oil it and sprinkle it with cornmeal.

5. Transfer your bread dough (it will be soft) to a lightly floured board to form the loaves. Sprinkle a little flour on it.

6. Cut the dough into 2 portions and roll each portion into a 12 to 15-inch wide rectangle (add more flour if required).

7. Roll up, pinching the seams well, starting from the long end. With the next roll, repeat the same process.

8. Place loaves of bread on a baking sheet that has been prepared; cover with a clean dishtowel and let rise for another hour.

9. Preheat your baking oven to 400 °F while the loaves are rising. Onto the last rack of the oven, put a pie plate, and add approximately 1 inch of boiling water to the pie plate. For 15 minutes, bake the bread.

10. Drop the heat to 350 °F and bake until golden brown for another 25 minutes.

11. Mix the egg white and cold water in a small bowl for about 5 minutes until the loaves are finished and rinse the loaves with the egg wash.

12. Remove from the oven until cooked and leave to cool.

13. Serve and enjoy.

3.5 Bread Machine Caramelized-Onion Bread

Total time

3 hours 40 minutes

Servings

12 servings

Nutrition facts

160 calories per serving

Ingredients

Here is the list of ingredients required to make caramelized onion bread.

- 3 cups bread flour

- 2 tbsp. sugar

- 1 tbsp. olive oil

- 1¼ tsp active dry yeast

- 1 tsp. salt

- 1 cup water

- 1 tbsp. butter

- 2 medium onions, caramelized

Method

Follow the instructions below to make caramelized-onion bread.

1. Melt butter over medium-low heat in a 10-inch pan. Cook onions in butter, stirring regularly, for 10 to 15 minutes, until they are brown. Remove the caramelized onions from the heat.

2. Measure carefully and put all the ingredients except the caramelized onions in the order suggested by the maker, in the bread machine tray. At the Raisin/Nut signal, add 1/2 cup of onions, or 5 to 10 minutes before the last kneading period

stops.

3. Reserve any leftover onions for another use.

4. Select the basic cycle of dough with medium or light crust.

5. Remove the baked bread from the pan; cool on the cooling rack.

3.6 Braided Onion-Potato Loaf

Total time

45 minutes

Servings

16 servings

Nutrition facts

130 calories per serving

Ingredients

Here is the list of ingredients required to make a braided onion potato loaf.

- 4 cups bread flour

- 1 large potato (peeled and cubed)

- 1 cup lukewarm milk

- 1 small onion (chopped)

- 1 large egg

- 1 tbsp. honey

- 2 tbsp. butter

- ¼ cup Parmesan cheese (grated)

- ¼ cup fresh parsley (chopped)

- 1 ½ tsp. salt

- 1½ tsp. active dry yeast

- ¼ tsp. pepper

- 1 large egg (beaten)

Method

Follow the instructions below to make a braided onion-potato loaf.

1. In a small saucepan put some water and add the onion and potatoes in it. Just bring it to a boil. Reduce heat; cover and cook for 10 to 15 minutes or until tender. Drain; mash until smooth (about 3/4 cup), set aside.

2. Add the mashed potato mixture, egg, milk, honey, cheese, butter, salt, pepper, parsley, yeast, and flour in the pan of the bread machine. Select Dough setting and start the machine. (Check the dough after kneading for five minutes. Adjust water or flour if required).

3. Turn the dough onto a lightly floured surface when the cycle is completed. Divide the dough into three parts. Shape them into an 18 inches rope, each. Place ropes of the dough on a greased baking sheet and braid; seal and tuck under by pinching ends.

4. Cover with a clean kitchen towel and let rise until doubled, about 1 hour, in a warm place. Uncover; top with a beaten egg brush. Add additional cheese to sprinkle. Bake onion-potato loaf for 25-35 minutes at 350° or until golden brown. Remove the baked bread from the pan to a cooling rack.

5. Serve and enjoy.

3.7 Sun-Dried Tomato & Olive Loaf

Total time

40 minutes

Servings

16 servings

Nutrition facts

126 calories per serving

Ingredients

Here is the list of ingredients required to make sun-dried tomato and olive loaf.

- 1 cup warm tomato juice

- 2 ¾ cups bread flour

- ½ tsp. salt

- 1 tsp. crushed dried rosemary or 1 tbsp. chopped fresh rosemary

- 2 tsp. brown sugar

- ½ cup sun-dried tomatoes(chopped)

- 2 tbsp. olive oil

- ½ Greek olives (chopped)

- 1 ½ tsp. instant yeast

Method

Follow the instructions below to make Sun-Dried tomato and olives bread.

1. Put the flour, 1tbsp. oil, brown sugar, rosemary, salt, tomato juice, 1 tbsp. oil, and yeast in the bread machine pan in the order recommended by the maker. Select the setting for the dough. When the dough is mixed for 5 minutes, check it; add 1-2 tablespoons of water or flour if needed. Add the tomatoes and olives just before the final kneading (your machine can audibly signal this).

2. Turn the dough onto a gently floured surface when the cycle is finished. Roll it into a 15*10 inches pan. Starting from a long side, roll up jelly-roll style; pinch seam to seal and tuck ends under. Place the seam side of bread down, on a greased baking sheet. Cover with a kitchen towel; let rise until doubled, about 45 minutes, in a warm place. Preheat your oven to 400 °.

3. Brush the loaf with the oil that remains. Create 5 deep slashes through the top of the loaf with a sharp knife. Bake until golden brown or 20-25 minutes. To cool, remove it from the pan to a wire rack.

3.8 French Baguettes

Total time

1 hour 50 minutes

Servings

12 servings

Nutrition facts

113 calories per serving

Ingredients

Here is the list of ingredients required to make French baguettes.

- 2 ½ cups bread flour

- 1 cup water

- 1 tbsp. white sugar

- 1 ½ tsp. bread machine yeast

- 1 egg yolk

- 1 tsp. salt

- 1 tbsp. water

Method

Follow the instructions below to prepare French baguettes.

1. Collect all the ingredients.

2. Add the bread flour, salt, sugar, and yeast into the bread machine pan in the order recommended by the bread machine manufacturer.

3. Select the dough cycle in the settings and then start the machine.

4. Place the dough in a greased bowl when the cycle has ended, spinning it to cover both sides. Cover the dough formed and allow it to rise for around 30

minutes in a warm place, or until doubled in size. If the indentation persists when touched, the

the dough is ready.

5. Punch the dough down. Roll into a 16*12 inches rectangle on a thinly floured surface. Halve the dough and make two 8*12 inches rectangles. Roll up each half of the dough firmly, pounding out any air bubbles as you go, starting at the 12-inch side. Roll slowly back and forth at the end of the taper. On a greased baking sheet, set 3 inches apart. Create deep diagonal slashes every 2 inches around the loaves, or make one slash on each loaf lengthwise. Cover, and allow it to rise for almost 30 to 40 minutes in a warm place, or until doubled in size.

6. The oven should be preheated to 375°F Mix 1 tbsp. of water with the egg yolk and brush it on the top of the loaf.

7. Bake in the preheated oven for 20 to 25 minutes, or until golden brown.

8. Serve and enjoy.

3.9 Bread Machine Focaccia Recipe

Total time

2 hours 20 minutes

Servings

8 servings

Nutrition facts

214 calories per serving

Ingredients

- 3 cups all-purpose flour

- 1 tsp. salt

- 1 cup water, warm water

- 1 tbsp. honey

- 2 tbsp. olive oil

- 2 ¼ tsp. bread machine yeast

- 1 tsp. sugar

Method

Follow the instructions below to prepare focaccia bread in the bread machine.

1. In the order given, add the ingredients to the bread machine. Start the cycle of dough. Take out the bread from the machine and put it on a floured surface. Divide in half and shape into two flat balls. Let them rest for about 10 minutes.

2. Take a deep dish pizza pan or thick baking sheet at least 13-inches. Generously apply some oil to the dish. If you are using your hands to flatten the dough, put the dough in a pan and flatten it.

3. For 30-40 minutes, let the dough rise. To poke random holes in the dough surface, use your fingertips.

4. Sprinkle the top with 1 tbsp. of olive oil, and then apply 1 tsp. of freshly ground pepper and fresh rosemary. Sprinkle on top some finely grated Parmesan Cheese.

5. 5. Bake for 8-10 minutes at 425 °F.

3.10 Papa Drexler's Bavarian Pretzels

Total time

35 minutes

Servings

6 servings

Nutrition facts

304 calories per serving

Ingredients

Here is the list of ingredients required to make these rolls.

- 3 cups all-purpose flour

- 1 tsp. white sugar

- 1 tbsp. active dry yeast

- 1 ⅓ cups water

- 3 tbsp. baking soda

- 1 tbsp. coarse sea salt, or to taste

- 2 tbsp. butter, melted

- 3 cups water

- 1 tbsp. coarse sea salt, or to taste

- 2 tbsp. butter softened

- 1 ⅓ cups water

- ¼ tsp. salt

- 3 tbsp. baking soda

- 3 cups water

- 2 tbsp. butter, melted

- 1 tbsp. sea salt

Method

Follow the instructions below to prepare these pretzels in the bread machine.

1. Stir 1 cup of flour, 2 tbsp. of butter, yeast, sugar, and 1 1/3 cup of water together in a wide bowl. Let this mixture stand for about 15 minutes before the bubble starts to form. Stir in the salt and steadily add the remaining flour until it is possible to pick up the dough and knead it on the table. Knead for around 8 minutes, until smooth and elastic, adding more flour as needed.

2. Divide the 6 parts of dough and let them sit for a few minutes. One part of the dough should be rolled at a time into a 15-inch-long rope. Loop and curl into the form of the cool pretzel. Set the remaining pieces on a baking sheet as you roll them out.

3. Preheat your oven to 450°F. Put to a boil the 3 remaining cups of water and add the baking soda. Remove the mixture from the heat. For about 45 seconds, dip the pretzels into the water bath, turning over about halfway through. On a greased baking sheet, put the soaked pretzels. Using melted butter to wash them and dust them with coarse salt.

4. Bake the pretzels in preheated oven for about 8 to 10 minutes or until golden brown.

3.11 Sour Cream Chive Bread

Total time

3 hours 10 minutes

Servings

16 servings

Nutrition facts

105 calories per serving

Ingredients

Here is the list of ingredients required to make sour cream chive bread.

- 1 cup warm milk

- ¼ cup lukewarm water

- ¼ cup sour cream

- 2 tsp. sugar

- 2 tbsp. butter

- 1 ½ tsp. salt

- 3 cups bread flour

- ¼ cup minced chives

- 2 ¼ teaspoons active dry yeast

- 1/8 tsp. baking soda

Method

Follow the instructions below to prepare this sour cream chive bread.

1. Collect all the ingredients

2. Add all ingredients in the order suggested by the manufacturer in the bread machine bowl. Select the simple setting for the bread. If available, choose the crust color and loaf size. Bake according to the instructions for bread machines.

After 5 minutes of mixing of dough check it and add 1 to 2 tbsp. of water if required.

3. When the bread is baked transfer it to a cooling rack and lets it cool properly.

4. Serve and enjoy.

3.12 Easy homemade French bread

Total time

1 hour 40 minutes

Servings

8 servings

Nutrition facts

210 calories per serving

Ingredients

Here is the list of ingredients required to make easy French bread.

- 1 ¼ cups hot water

- 1 tsp. salt

- 3 ½ cups bread flour

- 2 ¼ tsp. active dry yeast

- 1 tbsp. water

- 1 large egg

Method

Follow the instructions below to make easy French bread.

1. In your bread machine, place the above ingredients according to the manufacturer's instructions

2. Start the Dough Setting of your Machine

3. Preheat the oven to 175° F (you will transfer the loaves to the preheated oven for rising)

4. Switch off the oven when it reaches the required temperature

5. Divide the dough in half and roll each dough ballot about 12 inches long in french bread shape

6. Cut three thin slices of bread on top and put the loaves on a greased baking dish

7. Cover the dish and put it in the warmed oven

8. Leave the loaves to rise for about an hour, till they have doubled

9. Remove the loaves and preheat the oven to 450°F

10. Make an egg wash to have a perfect golden color on top of the bread. Mix one tablespoon of water with an egg together and whisk together very nice. Before baking the bread gently brush this egg wash on top of the bread

11. Bake the loaves until golden brown for 15-20 minutes, rotating the pan halfway around once during the baking process.

12. When done baking, remove loaves and allow to cool on wire racks.

Chapter 4: Cheese Bread recipes

4.1 Bread machine Basic cheese bread

Total time

3 hours 10 minutes

Servings

20 servings

Nutrition facts

196 calories per serving

Ingredients

Here is the list of ingredients required to make sour cream chive bread.

- 3 cups bread flour

- 1 cup warm water

- 2 cups shredded cheese

- ½ cup unsalted butter, melted

- 2 tsp. granulated sugar

- 1 ½ tsp. bread machine yeast

- 1 ½ tsp. coarse kosher salt

Method

Follow the instructions below to prepare this cheese bread in a bread machine.

1. Place the warm water, sugar, melted butter, and kosher salt in the pan of your bread machine. On top of the water mixture, add the shredded cheese and then add flour over the cheese.

2. Sprinkle the yeast, removing water spots if there are any on top of the flour base.

3. Put the baking pan in the bread machine and adjust the settings of the machine to Basic, medium crust, and 2 lb. loaf.

4. When the bread is baked transfer it to a cooling rack.

5. Allow the bread to cool for 10 minutes before cutting the slices, or to cool at room temperature before storage.

4.2 Pepperoni Cheese Bread

Total time

4 hour 10 minutes

Servings

16 servings

Nutrition facts

177 calories per serving

Ingredients

Here is the list of ingredients required to make Kalamata olive bread.

- 3 cups bread flour
- 1 ½ cups Mexican cheese (shredded)
- 1 cup lukewarm water
- 2 tsp. ground mustard
- 1 tbsp. butter
- 2 tbsp. sugar
- ½ tsp. cayenne pepper
- ½ tsp. salt
- 1 cup chopped pepperoni
- ¼ tsp. garlic powder
- 2 ¼ tsp. active dry yeast

Method

Follow the instructions below to prepare the pepperoni cheese bread.

1. Place all the ingredients in the bread machine pan except for cheese and pepperoni in the order recommended by the manufacturer.

2. Select the simple setting for the bread.

3. If available, choose the crust color and loaf size.

4. For the first five minutes of mixing, keep an eye on the dough by adding more water if it is stiff and crumbly and more flour if it is too wet.

5. Add the pepperoni and cheese just before the final kneading (your machine will audibly signal this).

6. Bake according to the instructions for bread machines.

7. If you want to freeze the bread then seal the cooled loaf tightly in foil and put it in a freezer bag.

4.3 Italian Cheese Bread

Total time

3 hours 10 minutes

Servings

12 servings

Nutrition facts

137calories per serving

Ingredients

Here is the list of ingredients required to make Italian cheese bread.

- 3 cups bread flour

- 2 tbsp. parmesan cheese (grated)

- 1 ¼ cups water

- ½ cup pepper jack cheese(shredded)

- 1 tsp. ground black pepper

- 2 tbsp. brown sugar

- 2 tsp. Italian seasoning

- 1 ½ tsp. salt

- 2 tsp. active dry yeast

Method

Follow the instructions below to make Italian cheese bread.

1. Collect all the ingredients.

2. Combine all the ingredients except cheese in the order recommended by the manufacturer in a bread machine pan. Select the simple setting for the bread. At the Raisin/Nut signal, add pepper jack and parmesan cheese 5 to 10 minutes before the last kneading period stops.

3. Choose the crust color and loaf size. Bake according to the instructions for bread machines. After mixing for 5 minutes check the dough and add 1 to 2 tbsp. of water if required.

4. When the bread is baked transfer it to a cooling rack.

5. Slice and enjoy.

4.4 Bread Machine Olive-Parmesan Bread

Total time

4 hours 10 minutes

Servings

12 servings

Nutrition facts

170 calories per serving

Ingredients

Here is the list of ingredients required to make Olive- Parmesan bread.

- 1 cup + 2 tbsp. water

- 3 cups bread flour

- 1 tbsp. sugar

- 2 tbsp. dry milk powder

- ¼ tsp. garlic powder

- 1 tbsp. sugar

- 2 tbsp. bread machine yeast

- 1 can of olives (sliced)

- 1 cup parmesan cheese (grated)

Method

Follow the instructions below to make olive-parmesan bread.

1. Collect all the ingredients.

2. Combine all the ingredients except olives and cheese in the order recommended by the manufacturer in a bread machine pan. Select the simple setting for the bread. At the Raisin/Nut signal, add 1 cup of cheese and olives 5 to 10 minutes before the

last kneading period stops.

3. Choose the crust color and loaf size. Bake according to the instructions for bread machines. After mixing for 5 minutes check the dough and add 1 to 2 tbsp. of water if required.

4. When the bread is baked transfer it to a cooling rack.

5. Slice and enjoy.

4.5 Bread Machine Cheddar and Bacon Bread Recipe

Total time

2 hours 50 minutes

Servings

10 servings

Nutrition facts

330 calories per serving

Ingredients

Here is the list of ingredients required to make cheddar and bacon bread.

- 4 cups bread flour

- 2 cups cheddar cheese (shredded)

- 3 tbsp. dry milk

- 2 tbsp. + 1 tbsp. sugar

- 1 ½ cups water

- 1 ¼ tsp. salt

- 2 tbsp. vegetable oil

- 2 tsp. active dry yeast

- 8 slices of bacon

Method

Follow the instructions below to make a cheddar and bacon bread recipe.

1. Collect all the ingredients.

2. Add the above ingredients into the bread machine pan in the order recommended by the bread machine manufacturer.

3. Select the basic cycle and choose medium crust in settings.

4. The oven should be preheated to 350 °F.

5. Bake the bread in your oven for 30-40 minutes or until the bread is golden brown.

6. Serve warm and enjoy.

4.6 Bread Machine Oregano and Romano Cheese Bread

Total time

2 hours 10 minutes

Servings

16 servings

Nutrition facts

61 calories per serving

Ingredients

Here is the list of ingredients required to make oregano and Romano cheese bread.

- 1 cup water

- 3 cups bread flour

- 3 tbsp. sugar

- 1 ½ tbsp. olive oil

- ½ cup Romano cheese

- 1 tbsp. dried oregano

- 2 tsp. dried yeast

- 1 tsp. salt

Method

Follow the instructions below to make oregano and Romano cheese bread.

1. Using the dough method, bake the bread in the bread machine.

2. Remove the machine's dough and turn it into a round loaf.

3. Place the loaf of bread on a baking sheet lined with parchment paper and cover it

with a damp kitchen towel.

4. Let it rise for 40 to 50 minutes until it has doubled.

5. Bake for 25 to 30 minutes or until golden brown in a preheated 400 °F oven.

4.7 Bread Machine Beer Cheese Bread

Total time

2 hours 10 minutes

Servings

10 servings

Nutrition facts

121 calories per serving

Ingredients

Here is the list of ingredients required to make beer cheese bread.

- 3 cups bread flour

- 2 ½ tsp. active dry yeast

- 1 ½ tsp. salt

- 1 tbsp. butter

- 1 ¼ cup beer

- 1 tbsp. sugar

- ½ cup American cheese

- ½ cup Monterey cheese

Method

Follow the instructions below to make beer cheese bread.

1. Heat the American cheese and beer together on the stovetop or in the microwave until just warm. Don't melt the cheese. Stir the mixture to blend it well.

2. Shift the mixture to the machine pan to make the bread. If it seems too hot, let the mixture cool down until it's warm.

3. Add the remaining ingredients into the pan and choose a simple setting or white bread, and press the Start button.

4.8 Pepper Jack Cheese Bread

Total time

2 hours 15 minutes

Servings

16 servings

Nutrition facts

110 calories per serving

Ingredients

Here is the list of ingredients required to make pepper jack cheese bread.

- 2 tbsp. olive oil

- 1 tsp. sugar

- 1 tbsp. active dry yeast

- 1 tbsp. Italian seasoning

- 1 cup lukewarm water

- ½ tsp. salt

- 1 tsp. garlic powder

- 3 cups bread flour

- ½ cup pepper jack cheese (cubed)

Method

Follow the instructions below to make pepper jack cheese bread.

1. Combine the sugar, water, and yeast in a mixing cup. Let it sit for 10 minutes or until it's frothy.

2. Add and mix all the remaining ingredients except the flour.

3. Add 1/2 cup of flour to the mixture at a time until it is no longer sticky.

4. Knead for around 7 minutes in the machine.

5. Use olive oil to lightly oil the bowl and let the dough rise for around 1 hour.

6. Your oven should be preheated to 425 °F.

7. Oil a baking sheet gently place the dough. Knead in the cheese inside the dough until the cubes are uniformly dispersed. Shape the dough on an oiled baking sheet into a loaf form. Let the loaf rise for 25 to 30 minutes.

8. Bake for 15 minutes or until golden brown on top.

4.9 Cheese herb bread recipe

Total time

3 hours

Servings

12 servings

Nutrition facts

163 calories per serving

Ingredients

Here is the list of ingredients required to make cheese and herb bread.

- 3 cups bread flour

- 2 tbsp. sugar

- 1 ½ tsp. salt

- 1 ¼ cups warm water

- 2 tbsp. dry milk

- 2 tbsp. butter (softened)

- 3 tbsp. parmesan cheese (grated)

- 1 ½ dried thyme

- 1 ½ tsp. dried marjoram

- 1 tsp. dried basil

- 1 tsp. dried oregano

- 1 tbsp. active dry yeast

Method

Follow the instructions below to make cheese and herb bread.

1. Collect all the ingredients.

2. Add the above ingredients into the bread machine pan in the order recommended by the bread machine manufacturer.

3. Select the basic cycle and choose medium crust in settings.

4. The oven should be preheated to 350 °F.

5. Bake the bread in your oven for 30-40 minutes or until the bread is golden brown.

6. Serve warm and enjoy.

4.10 Onion, Garlic, and Cheese Bread

Total time

3 hours 5 minutes

Servings

12 servings

Nutrition facts

205 calories per serving

Ingredients

Here is the list of ingredients required to make Onion, garlic, and cheese bread.

- 3 cups bread flour

- 2 tbsp. sugar

- 1 cup warm water

- 2 tbsp. dry milk powder

- 2 tbsp. butter

- 2 tsp. garlic powder

- 1 ½ tsp. salt

- 2 tsp. active dry yeast

- 3 tbsp. dried minced onion

- 2 tsp. garlic powder

- 1 cup cheddar cheese (shredded)

Method

Follow the instructions below to make onion, garlic cheese bread.

1. In the order recommended by your manufacturer, add water, flour, dry milk, butter or margarine sugar, salt, and yeast to the bread machine

2. Select the basic cycle of the machine and choose light crust.

3. Add 2 tablespoons of the onion flakes, the garlic powder, and all the shredded cheese when the alarm sound beeps or as suggested by the machine. The remaining tablespoon of onion flakes is sprinkled over the dough after the last knead.

4. Enjoy bread when it is hot and fresh

Chapter 5: Sweet Bread recipes

5.1 Sweet Banana Bread with Yeast

Total time

3 hours 15 minutes

Servings

16 servings

Nutrition facts

166 calories per serving

Ingredients

Here is the list of ingredients required to make sweet banana bread.

- ½ cup warm milk or yogurt

- 1 ¾ cup bread flour or all-purpose flour

- 1 large egg

- ½ tsp. salt

- 1 tbsp. honey

- 2 tbsp. butter

- 1 small ripe banana (mashed)

- 2 tsp. instant yeast or bread machine yeast

- 1 tbsp. milk

- 65 g toasted almonds or pecans

- 45g chopped dates

- 50 g raisins

- 1 tbsp. sugar

- ½ tsp. ground cardamom

Method

Follow the instructions below to prepare sweet banana bread with yeast in the bread machine.

1. In the order given, mix all of the dough ingredients (except the raisins, nuts, and dates) into the bread-machine tray. Set on the cycle of the dough. Add nuts and dried fruit as the machine signals it is time for "add-ins".

2. If the dough is doubled to its size at end of the dough cycle, then remove it from the pan but if it's not doubled then keep it in the machine until it has doubled. Remove to a surface that is gently floured and shape into a ball. Allow the ball of dough to rest for 10 minutes.

3. Divided into 3 separate parts. Form 3 cylinders about 12 inches long each. Braid the bread by tucking the ends.

4. Transfer to a silicone baking mat or parchment paper-covered cookie sheet. Let the soft tea towel cover the dough for about 45 minutes.

5. Roll the dough into three balls and put it in a loaf pan side by side.

6. Lightly brush milk over the raised bread. Combine the cardamom sugar and sprinkle over the braid.

7. Bake for 30-35 minutes at 375° F or until golden brown.

5.2 Pecan Raisin Bread

Total time

3 hours 10 minutes

Servings

16 servings

Nutrition facts

227 calories per serving

Ingredients

Here is the list of ingredients required to make yummy pecan raisin bread.

- 4 cups bread flour

- 8 tsp. butter

- 1 cup + 2 tbsp. warm water

- 1 egg room temperature

- ¼ cup nonfat dry milk powder

- 6 tbsp. sugar

- 1 tbsp. active dry yeast

- 1 tsp. salt

- 1 cup raisins

- 1 cup chopped pecans

Method

Follow the instructions below to prepare this pecan raisin bread.

1. Put the first eight ingredients in the bread machine pan in the order recommended by the maker. Select the simple setting for the bread. If available, choose the crust color and loaf size.

2. Bake according to the instructions of the bread machine. After five minutes of mixing

check the dough of bread and add 1 to 2 tbsp. of water if required.

3. Add pecans and raisins just before the final kneading.

4. Bake it for 3 hours in the oven or until done.

5. Take the bread out of the bread machine pan carefully and cool it on a wire rack.

6. Serve and Enjoy.

5.3 Bread Machine Coffee Cake

Total time

3 hours

Servings

16 servings

Nutrition facts

105 calories per serving

Ingredients

Here is the list of ingredients required to make a coffee cake in a bread machine.

- 2 cups all-purpose flour

- ⅓ cup instant potato flakes

- 2 tsp. instant yeast

- ⅓ cup softened butter unsalted

- ⅓ cup white sugar

- ½ cup + 2 tbsp. water

- ¾ tsp. salt

- ½ tsp. vanilla

- ¾ brown sugar

- 1 tsp. cinnamon

- ¼ cup butter melted

- ½ cup powdered sugar

- ½ tsp. vanilla extract

- 2 tsp. cream or milk

Method

Follow the instructions below to prepare this coffee cake in a bread machine.

1. In the order recommended by the manufacturer, add all the dough ingredients to your bread machine.

2. Select the dough cycle.

3. Check the dough's consistency as it kneads for the first five minutes, adding more water if the dough is stiff and crumbly or if it sticks, adding more flour. The dough so is smooth so that it clears the sides of the pan.

4. Once the machine beeps, take out the dough from the pan. It may have slightly risen.

5. Gently spread it in a 13*9 inches pan and cover the pan.

6. Place the pan in a warm place and let it rise for almost 1 hour.

7. The oven should be preheated to 350 °F.

8. Once the dough has risen, mix the sugar and cinnamon for topping.

9. Use your fingertips to make indentations in the dough and sprinkle the cinnamon sugar on top of the dough.

10. Add the melted butter on top of the dough and bake it for almost 25 to 30 minutes or until done.

11. Cool the bread in the pan slightly.

12. Mix butter, powdered sugar, vanilla extract, and cream to prepare the glaze and add it to the top of the cake.

13. Serve the cake and enjoy.

14. It will stay at room temperature for two days, tightly wrapped.

5.4 Sweet Strawberry Breakfast Bread

Total time

2 hours 50 minutes

Servings

16 servings

Nutrition facts

134 calories per serving

Ingredients

Here is the list of ingredients required to make sweet strawberry bread.

- 2 cups all-purpose flour

- ⅓ cup unsalted butter (softened)

- ⅓ cup potato flakes

- 2 tsp. instant yeast

- ½ cup water

- ⅓ cup white sugar

- ½ tsp. vanilla

- ¾ tsp. salt

- 2 tbsp. Strawberry Jam

- ½ cup powdered sugar

- ½ tsp. of vanilla extract

- 2 teaspoons cream or milk

Method

Follow the instructions below to prepare this sweet strawberry bread in a bread machine.

1. Mix all the ingredients in a bread machine in the order suggested by the manufacturer

2. Change the settings to dough cycle and start the machine.

3. When the dough cycle is completed and the machine beeps, check the consistency of the dough. Your dough should be soft and smooth and slightly sticky if you touch it but make sure that the bread machine pan is cleared from sides and bottom with no residue left.

4. Use cooking oil spray or butter to prepare a 9*13 inches casserole dish. Spread the dough in the pan. Cover the dough with some foil and allow it to rise in a warm position for 1 hour. You can also place it in the fridge overnight.

5. When the dough has risen, spread some strawberry jam on it.

6. Bake for 25-30 minutes at 350 °F. It should be slightly brown from the edges.

7. Once the strawberry bread is baked, remove it from the oven and cool it on a cooling rack for about 1 hour.

8. Mix the glaze; it should not be too runny and easily pourable.

9. Serve directly from the pan.

5.5 Hawaiian Bread Recipe for Bread Machine

Total time

3 hours 45 minutes

Servings

12 servings

Nutrition facts

170 calories per serving

Ingredients

Here is the list of ingredients required to make sweet strawberry bread.

- 3 cups bread flour

- ¾ cup lukewarm milk

- 1 ½ tbsp. butter (softened)

- ¼ cup potato flakes

- ¼ cup to ½ cup pineapple juice

- 1 ½ tbsp. salt

- 2 tsp. instant yeast

- 1 ½ tbsp. sugar

Method

Follow the instructions below to prepare Hawaiian bread.

1. Combine all the ingredients in the pan of the bread machine.

2. Select the dough cycle.

3. Mix and check after a few minutes to make sure the dough is not too dry or too wet. It should be soft and smooth, but the bowl's sides should still be clear.

4. Take the kneaded dough out of the bowl and put it on the counter or cutting board. Shape into a rectangle that is the same size as your loaf pan to form into a sandwich

loaf. Fold the seams into thirds, pinching. Tuck the ends underneath and flip the loaf over so that on the bottom is the seam. Place it in a greased loaf pan.

5. With greased plastic wrap, cover the dough and place it in a warm place to rise. The dough should rise almost 1 ½ inch. Brush the beaten egg over the dough.

6. Preheat the oven to 350 °F.

7. Place the pan in the middle rack and bake until the loaf is golden brown, almost for 40-50 minutes. The internal temperature of the bread should be 195-200 °.

8. Allow it to completely cool on the wire rack. Slice when perfectly cool. It can be consumed within 2-3 days at room temperature.

9. Serve and enjoy.

5.6 Honey bread recipe

Total time

3 hours 5 minutes

Servings

10 servings

Nutrition facts

165 calories per serving

Ingredients

Here is the list of ingredients required to make honey bread.

- 1½ cups whole wheat flour

- 1 cup warm water

- 2 tbsp. honey

- 2 tbsp. butter(softened)

- 1 tsp. Himalayan salt

- 2 tsp. bread machine yeast

- 1½ cups unbleached flour

Method

Follow the instructions below to make a honey bread recipe.

1. To the bread machine's baking pan, add butter, butter, warm water, honey, and salt.

2. Add the flour to the pan and sprinkle the yeast on top of the mixture.

3. Place the baking pan back to the bread machine.

4. Set the machine to dough cycle and change settings to 1.5lbs and medium crust.

5. Before cutting, allow the bread to cool down.

6. Serve and enjoy.

5.7 Lemon Bread Recipe

Total time

4 hours 15 minutes

Servings

12 servings

Nutrition facts

260 calories per serving

Ingredients

Here is the list of ingredients required to make lemon bread.

- 3 ¼ cups flour

- ½ cup milk

- 1 tsp. salt

- ¼ cup sugar

- 2 large eggs

- 2 large eggs

- ¼ cup butter (softened)

- Lemon zest of 3 lemons

- 1/4 cup melted butter

- Orange zest of 1 orange

- ½ cup sugar

- 1 cup (227 grams) powdered sugar

- 2 tbsp. of cream or milk

Method

Follow the instructions below to make lemon bread.

1. Place the first 7 ingredients in the order specified in the bread machine pan. Choosing the dough cycle, start the machine. Open the lid after 5 minutes and check the dough. It's meant to hold to its side of the pan if it is so then pull away. If the dough is too stiff start adding milk, one tablespoon at a time. Add flour one tablespoon at a time if it is too wet.

2. Remove the dough to a floured surface, when the dough cycle completes (dough should be doubled in size at this point) and roll into a rectangle about 8*10 inches in size.

3. Divide the dough into large diamonds using a pizza cutter or knife.

4. In the melted butter dip each diamond and then coat it with a mixture of sugary lemon/orange zest.

5. Place the first piece in the Bundt Pan on its side. Lay the second piece upright against the first piece, and then repeat until the pan is lined up with all the pieces. In the final pieces, you will have to press them together to pinch. Perfection is not mandatory.

6. Cover with a shower cap, plastic wrap, or tea towel and allow it to rise until nearly double in a warm place.

7. Uncover and bake for 30-35 minutes or until the internal temperature exceeds 190 °F in an oven preheated to 350 degrees F. To avoid the crush to be over-browned use an aluminum sheet to cover the loaf pan between baking period.

8. Enable 5 minutes to cool before taking it out of the pan. Turn it upside down so you can see the crusty top.

9. Mix the powdered sugar with cream or milk and it drizzle over the top while the bread is still warm.

5.8 Bread Machine Apple Cider Cinnamon Bread

Total time

3hours 38 minutes

Servings

16 servings

Nutrition facts

120 calories per serving

Ingredients

Here is the list of ingredients required to make 50% whole wheat bread.

- 3 cups bread flour

- 2 tbsp. brown sugar

- 1 ¼ cup apple cider vinegar

- 2 tbsp. butter (softened)

- 1 tsp. ground cinnamon

- 1 tsp. salt

- 2 ¼ tsp. active dry yeast

Method

Follow the instructions below to make Apple Cider Cinnamon bead.

1. In the order suggested by your machine maker, mix the ingredients in the bread machine.

2. Choose the setting for white bread with a light brown crust.

3. Remove the pan from the bread machine when the baking period finishes and allow it to cool for 10 minutes.

4. Remove the bread from the pan and let it cool entirely before slicing by placing it on a wire rack.

5. Store the bread in an airtight jar at room temperature.

5.9 Rosemary Bread with Dried Cranberries and Pecans

Total time

3hours 30minutes

Servings

12 servings

Nutrition facts

129 calories per serving

Ingredients

Here is the list of ingredients required to make rosemary bread with dried cranberries and pecans.

- 1 1/12 cups unbleached flour

- 1 tsp. instant yeast

- 1 cup cold water

- 3 tbsp. water

- 2 cups all-purpose flour

- 1 ½ tsp. salt

- Pre-ferment mixture

- 1 tsp. sugar

- ½ cup toasted pecans (chopped)

- 2 tsp. fresh rosemary (chopped)

- 1 cup dried cranberries

Method

Follow the instructions below to make rosemary bread with cranberries and pecans.

1. In the bread machine pan, put the first three ingredients (yeast, water, and flour). Select the "dough" cycle. Use a small spatula to carefully push the flour stuck in the

corners into the mixing area and allow it to mix for about 5 minutes.

2. Unplug the machine and let it rest overnight or for about 8 hours at room temperature. Do not leave it for more than 16 hours.

3. Pre-ferment is ready after 8 hours.

4. Add flour, salt, water, and sugar to pre-ferment.

5. Now start the dough cycle again.

6. After 10-15 minutes of mixing, check the dough. If required, add 1 tablespoon of additional flour at a time to create a smooth yet slightly tacky ball. If the dough is too stiff and bounces against the edges, apply water, 1 tablespoon at a time.

7. Add rosemary, cherries, and pecans when the machine beeps.

8. Let the dough rise in the process for at least 30 minutes (or longer if the air temperature is cool) until it has doubled in size when the dough cycle stops.

9. Transfer the dough to a thinly floured board or silicone baking mat from the bread-machine tray

10. Roll roughly 8 x 12 inches of dough into an oblong shape. Rollback it again beginning from the long side. Together, pinch a seam. Switch under the ends and pinch them together. Manipulate the shape into a rounded rectangle.

11. Place the dough rectangles on a cookie sheet covered with parchment. With lightly-oiled plastic wrap, cover loosely and put in a warm place for rising until almost double.

12. Preheat the oven to 425 °F for about 15 minutes until the bread is ready to bake.

13. Sprinkle the top with flour before putting the bread in the oven. Make multiple cuts over the top of bread about 1/2 inches deep using a single-edge razor blade (or a sharp knife).

14. Bake for almost 30 to 35 minutes so the loaf turns to golden brown and the internal the temperature of the bread reaches 190 ° F.

15. Let the bread cool on a wire rack.

16. Slice and enjoy.

5.10 Bread Machine Pumpkin Yeast Bread

Total time

3 hours 5 minutes

Servings

4 servings

Nutrition facts

226 calories per serving

Ingredients

Here is the list of ingredients required to make pumpkin yeast bread.

- 4 cups bread flour

- 1 cup pumpkin puree or mashed pumpkin

- 2 tbsp. vegetable oil

- 1 ¼ tsp. salt

- 2 ¼ tsp. active dry yeast

- 2 tbsp. sugar

- ½ cup + 2 tbsp. milk

Method

Follow the instructions below to make pumpkin yeast bread.

1. In the order suggested by your machine maker, mix the ingredients in the bread machine.

2. Choose the setting for basic bread with a light brown crust.

3. Remove the pan from the bread machine when the baking period finishes and allow

it to cool for 10 minutes.

4. Remove the bread from the pan and let it cool entirely before slicing by placing it on a wire rack.

5. Store the bread in an airtight jar at room temperature.

5.11 Bread Machine Cardamom Bread

Total time

2 hours 45 minutes

Servings

12 servings

Nutrition facts

163calories per serving

Ingredients

Here is the list of ingredients required to make cardamom bread.

- ¼ cup honey

- ½ cup milk

- ¼ cup apple sauce (unsweetened)

- 1 egg

- ¼ tsp. salt

- 3 cups bread flour

- 2 tsp. active dry yeast

- ½ tsp cardamom powder

Method

Follow the instructions below to make cardamom bread.

1. In the order suggested by the manufacturer, put the ingredients in the pan of your bread machine. Click Start and choose the Dough Cycle.

2. Remove the dough, and then knead gently when the bread maker signals that the cycle has stopped. Shape the dough into the form of a loaf, and put it into a 9x5 inch greased bread tray. Cover, and let rise for about 45 minutes until doubled in size, in a warm spot.

3. Your oven should be preheated to 350 °F.

4. Uncover the loaf, and use water to brush the surface of the loaf. Bake the cardamom bread in preheated oven for 40 to 45 minutes or until nicely browned, and when tapped on the rim, the loaf produces a hollow sound. Enable to cool before removing from the pan for 10 minutes. Before slicing, chill for around 1 hour.

5.12 Bread Machine Almond Bread

Total time

3 hours 10 minutes

Servings

12 servings

Nutrition facts

117calories per serving

Ingredients

Here is the list of ingredients required to make almond bread.

- 4 tbsp. almond oil

- ¼ cup honey

- 1 cup almond flour

- ¼ cup wheat gluten

- 2 cups whole wheat flour

- 1 tsp. salt

- 1 tsp. xanthan gum

- 2 ½ tsp. active dry yeast

Method

Follow the instructions below to make Almond bread.

1. Mix water, almond flour, salt, wheat flour, xanthan gum, almond oil, honey, vital wheat gluten, and yeast, respectively into the bread machine pan. Follow the recommended manufacturers' instructions for a 2 lb. loaf.

5.13 Bread Machine Glazed Yeast Doughnuts

Total time

10 hours 35 minutes

Servings

24 servings

Nutrition facts

269 calories per serving

Ingredients

Here is the list of ingredients required to make glazed doughnuts.

- ½ cup water
- 3 cups all-purpose flour
- ½ cup evaporated milk
- 2 tbsp. butter
- ½ cup sugar
- 1 tsp. salt
- 1 egg beaten
- 2 tsp. active dry yeast
- Oil (for deep frying)
- 2 tbsp. cocoa
- 1 ½ cups powdered sugar
- 2 tbsp. butter
- 3 tbsp. hot water
- ½ tsp. vanilla extract

Method

Follow the instructions below to make Glazed Doughnuts.

1. Use the bread machine and add all the ingredients to the pan. Cover the pan with plastic wrap at the end of the kneading period, and move it to the refrigerator. (Or, into a lightly greased bowl, shift the mixture)

2. Refrigerate the dough overnight.

3. Remove the dough to a thinly floured surface and roll to a thickness of around 1/2-inch.

4. Cut out the shape of doughnuts from the dough with a help of a cutter.

5. Cover and let rise for approximately 1 hour.

6. Fry at 360 ° F in oil until light and brown.

7. Melt butter in a small saucepan. The flame should be medium to low. Add cocoa and water.

8. Stir continually until the mixture is dense.

9. Remove the mixture from heat; add powdered sugar and vanilla gradually; beat until smooth with a whisk.

10. Up to the desire drizzling consistency add hot water.

11. Once the glaze is ready coat your doughnuts in it from the top.

5.14 Bread Machine Chocolate Bread

Total time

6 hours 10 minutes

Servings

8 servings

Nutrition facts

256 calories per serving

Ingredients

Here is the list of ingredients required to make chocolate bread.

- 3 cups bread flour

- 1 cup lukewarm milk

- 3 tbsp. canola oil

- 1 tsp. salt

- 1 egg + 1 yolk

- 1 tsp. vanilla extract

- ½ cup brown sugar

- 1 tbsp. wheat gluten

- ½ cup chocolate powder

- 2 ½ tsp. bread machine yeast

Method

Follow the instructions below to make chocolate bread.

1. Collect all the ingredients.

2. Add the above ingredients into the bread machine pan in the order recommended by the bread machine manufacturer.

3. Select the basic cycle and choose medium crust in settings.

4. The oven should be preheated to 350 °F.

5. Bake the bread for 30-40 minutes or until the bread is golden brown.

6. Serve warm and enjoy.

5. 15 Banana Raisin Bread

Total time

4 hours 10 minutes

Servings

16 servings

Nutrition facts

207 calories per serving

Ingredients

Here is the list of ingredients required to make banana raisin bread.

- 3 tbsp. honey

- 1 egg yolk (lightly beaten)

- 4 ½ tsp. vegetable oil

- 1 medium ripe banana (mashed)

- ½ cup + 2 tbsp. water

- 1 12 tsp. active dry yeast

- 1 tsp. salt

- 1tsp. ground cinnamon

- 1 cup chopped walnuts

- ½ cup raisins

Method

Follow the instructions below to make Banana Raisin bread.

1. Collect all the ingredients.

2. Combine all the ingredients except walnuts and raisins in the order recommended

by the manufacturer in a bread machine pan.

3. Select the simple setting for the bread.

4. After mixing for 5 minutes check the dough and add 1 to 2 tbsp. of water if required.

5. At the Raisin/Nut signal, add walnuts and raisins 5 to 10 minutes before the last kneading period stops.

6. Choose the crust color and loaf size. Bake according to the instructions for bread machines.

7. When the bread is baked transfer it to a cooling rack.

8. Slice and enjoy.

5.16 Bread Machine Saffron Bread

Total time

2 hours 10 minutes

Servings

12 servings

Nutrition facts

168 calories per serving

Ingredients

Here is the list of ingredients required to make saffron bread.

- 1 tbsp. butter (softened)

- 1 cup milk

- 2 eggs

- ½ cup sugar

- ¼ tsp. saffron powder

- 3 ¼ cups all-purpose flour

- 2 ½ tsp. yeast

- 1 tsp. salt

- 1 cup raisins

Method

Follow the instructions below to make Saffron bread.

1. Collect all the ingredients.

2. Combine all the ingredients except walnuts and raisins in the order recommended by the manufacturer in a bread machine pan.

3. Select the simple setting for the bread.

4. At the Raisin/Nut signal, add w raisins 5 to 10 minutes before the last kneading period stops.

5. Choose the crust color and loaf size. Bake according to the instructions for bread machines.

6. When the bread is baked transfer it to a cooling rack.

7. Slice and enjoy.

5.17 Bear Claws Pastry Recipe

Total time

3 hours

Servings

10 servings

Nutrition facts

582 calories per serving

Ingredients

Here is the list of ingredients required to make these pastries.

- 2 ¼ cup +1 tbsp. all-purpose flour

- ¼ cup sour cream

- ¼ cup sugar

- 2 tsp. bread machine yeast

- ¼ cup + 2 tbsp. butter (softened)

- ¼ cup warm water

- ½ tsp. salt

- 1 egg

- 1 tsp. cinnamon

- ¼ cup sugar

- 2 tsp. cream cheese

- 2 tsp. butter

- 1½ tbsp. Milk or coffee

- 1 cup powdered sugar

- ¼ cup sliced almonds (toasted)

- 1½ tbsp. Milk or coffee

Method

Follow the instructions below to prepare bear claw pastries in the bread machine.

1. In the order mentioned, add the dough ingredients to a bread machine pan. Set on the cycle of the dough. Remove the dough from the bread-machine pan when finished. Proceed to the directions below for Roll-out.

2. On a lightly floured board. Roll the dough into a rectangle measuring 6 x 24 inches.

3. On the rectangle, spread the softened butter. Generously sprinkle the cinnamon-sugar mixture evenly around the buttered surface.

4. From the long side, start rolling and roll up as tightly as possible. Slightly flatten the log with your hands and cut the log into 10 parts.

5. Make 2 cuts through each slice using a kitchen knife or sharp pizza cutter.

6. To make it lay much flatter, curl each slice slightly. Position the pastries on a greased baking sheet or one covered with a silicone mat or parchment paper.

7. For 15-20 minutes, bake the rolls at 375° F until golden brown.

8. Soften the butter and cream cheese and allow them to reach room temperature. Mix the butter, cream cheese, and coffee or milk, and beat until perfectly smooth.

9. To drizzle frosting over the rolls, use a spoon. Or pour the frosting into a small, zippered plastic bag. Cut off a tiny corner of the bag and drizzle the frosting back and forth over the rolls using the closed bag.

10. Immediately sprinkle the almonds on the top of frosted pastries before the frosting dries. Or hold the frosted pastry and turn it upside down into the almond tray pressing the icing on almonds. This means that the almonds will stick on the icing.

5.18 Fresh Blueberry Bread Machine Recipe

Total time

3 hours 45 minutes

Servings

12 servings

Nutrition facts

225 calories per serving

Ingredients

Here is the list of ingredients required to make Fresh blueberry bread.

- 1 ½ cup blueberries

- ¼ cup lukewarm water

- 3 large eggs

- ¼ cup heavy cream

- 1 tsp. salt

- 4 tbsp. + 2 tbsp. sugar

- ½ cup butter (cubed)

- 1 ½ cups + 3 tbsp. all-purpose flour

- 1 ½ cups bread flour

- 2 tsp. active dry yeast

- 1 tbsp. heavy cream

- Pinch of salt

- 1 egg

- Sugar for sprinkling

Method

Follow the instructions below to make fresh blueberry bread.

1. Before preparing the dough, drain fresh blueberries and place them on a paper towel to dry and reach room temperature.

2. Put the remaining ingredients into your bread machine's bread pan. Choose the duration of the dough and press start. After about 10-15 minutes of mixing, open the lid and check the dough to make sure the consistency is correct. It should stick to the side of the pan, then pull forward. If the dough is too stiff, add 1 teaspoonful of more water at a time. If it is too sticky, add 1 tablespoon of flour at a time.

3. Remove the dough to a floured surface when the dough cycle ends and the dough has risen to twice its original size. Press or roll about 10 x 16 inches of dough into a rectangle. The short side of the rectangle should be towards you.

4. Add the berries over the dough and then sprinkle about 2 tbsp. of sugar. To make a cylinder, gently roll the top of the dough towards you.

5. Turn the dough cylinder into 90° and roll it into a rectangle of around 12 x 6 inches. Tightly roll the dough from the top, with the short end nearest to you. Just seal the seam. With the seam side down, put in a greased 9 x 5-inch loaf tray.

6. Let it rise to almost twice its size. Depending on the air temperature, it can take 1 hour or more. About 1/2 inch of the dough should be peeking over the end.

7. Preheat your oven to 350° F when the bread has almost doubled.

8. In a small cup, combine the ingredients for the glaze. Brush the glaze with a soft touch to the unbaked loaf so the glaze would not puddle at the loaf's outer edges. Sprinkle plenty of sugar in it. You can use sugar sanding, but normal sugar also works.

9. Bake for 40-45 minutes at 350°. When the probe is placed into the center of the loaf, the temperature must read at least 190-200 ° F. Before the bread is finished baking, watch to ensure that the crust doesn't over-brown. To stop burning the crust, try covering the loaf halfway through the baking period with aluminum foil if necessary.

10. Cool for almost 15 minutes before removing from the pan and after that place it on a cooling rack for almost 1 hour,

11. Serve and enjoy.

Chapter 6: Bread Rolls recipes

6.1 Soft onion sandwich rolls with a bread machine

Total time

3 hours 20 minutes

Servings

8 servings

Nutrition facts

260 calories per serving

Ingredients

Here is the list of ingredients required to make these rolls.

- 3 cups all-purpose flour

- 3 tbsp. butter softened

- 1 ½ tsp. salt

- 3 tbsp. dried minced onion

- 1 tsp. onion powder

- 2 ½ tbsp. active dry yeast

- ¼ cup potato flakes

- 3 tbsp. white sugar

- ¾ cup lukewarm milk

- 5 tbsp. water

- 1 egg white

Method

Follow the instructions below to prepare these rolls in the bread machine.

1. In the order recommended by the maker, put the butter, water, milk, sugar, salt, 3 tablespoons of dried onion, onion powder, potato flakes, yeast, and flour in the pan of a bread machine. Choose the Dough Cycle and then push the Start button.

2. Remove the dough from the process and knead it on a gently floured surface when the cycle has ended. Divide into 8 pieces equal to each other, and shape into balls. Flatten the balls softly until they measure 4 inches in diameter. If they continue to shrink up, just let them rest before flattening for a minute. Place it on a baking sheet and use a towel to cover it loosely. Set to rise until doubled in size, around 40 minutes in a draft-free environment.

3. Your oven should be preheated to 350°F (175°C). Whisk the white egg and water together in a cup. Brush and sprinkle with the remaining minced onion over the tops of the raised rolls.

4. Bake in the preheated oven for 15 to 20 minutes, until golden brown. Cool perfectly and then horizontally slice in half before use.

5. Enjoy.

6.2 Bread Machine Hawaiian Sweet Rolls

Total time

2 hours 40 minutes

Servings

12

Nutrition Facts

212 calories per serving

Ingredients

Here is the list of ingredients required to make these rolls.

- ⅓ cup milk

- 1 cup pineapple juice

- 4 tbsp. unsalted butter

- 1 large egg

- 3 ½ cups bread flour

- 1 tsp. Coconut extract

- ½ cup dry potato flakes

- 1 ½ tsp. active dry yeast

- ⅓ cup white sugar

- 1 tsp. salt

- ⅓ tsp. ground ginger

Method

Follow the instructions below to prepare these rolls in the bread machine.

1. In a bread machine, put the milk, pineapple juice, butter, egg, coconut extract, potato flakes, bread flour, salt, sugar, yeast, and ginger in the order specified, or as instructed by the manufacturer. Run the dough cycle. Remove the dough for

around 1 hour after the cycle is over.

2. Shape the dough into rolls, placed it on a baking sheet, and let it rise for 1 hour.

3. Your oven should be preheated to 350°F (175° C).

4. Bake until golden, about 20 minutes, in the preheated oven.

6.3 Easy Bread Machine Sandwich Rolls

Total time

2 hours 35 minutes

Servings

12 servings

Nutrition facts

159 calories per serving

Ingredients

Here is the list of ingredients required to make these bread machine sandwich rolls.

- 4 cups all-purpose flour

- 2 tsp. salt

- 1 ½ cups water

- 1 tsp. sugar

- pinch of cornmeal

- 2 tsp. instant yeast

Method

Follow the instructions below to prepare these sandwich rolls.

1. In the order suggested by the manufacturer, add all the ingredients (except cornmeal) to the pan of a bread machine.

2. Change the settings to dough cycle and start the machine.

3. For the first five minutes of mixing, keep an eye on the dough by adding more water if it is stiff and crumbly and more flour if it is too wet.

4. When the dough cycle is completed and the machine beeps, check the consistency of the dough. Your dough should be soft and smooth and slightly sticky if you touch it but make sure that the bread machine pan is cleared from sides and

bottom with no residue left.

5. Cut the dough into twelve equal parts with a help of a sharp knife.

6. Shape softly into rolls to smooth out the tops by pressing down the bottoms of the dough.

7. Dust flour on top and rub it on the rolls.

8. Place a parchment paper on the baking tray and dust it with some cornmeal.

9. Now gently place the rolls on the baking tray and cover the tray with a greased plastic wrap.

10. Leave the rolls into a warm place for about 45 minutes or until they are fluffy.

11. Preheat your oven to 425 °F and pour one cup of water into the baking sheet to create steam.

12. Bake the rolls for around 15 to 20 minutes or until golden brown.

13. Once done, remove them from the oven and cool them on a cooling rack.

14. Eat warm as dinner rolls or cut them for sandwiches when cool.

15. Eat within 2 days.

6.4 Fluffy Bread Machine Rolls

Total time

1 hour 16 minutes

Servings

16 servings

Nutrition facts

183 calories per serving

Ingredients

Here is the list of ingredients required to make fluffy bread machine rolls.

- 3 cups bread flour

- 1¼ cup milk

- 2 tbsp. butter (melted)

- 1 tsp. salt

- 3 tbsp. sugar

- 2 ¼ active dry yeast

Method

Follow the instructions below to make fluffy bread rolls.

1. In the order recommended by your machine manufacturer, put all of the ingredients in the pan of your bread machine. Set the machine to dough cycle and push the start button.

2. Take the dough from the machine pan when the machine is done and put it on a floured surface, gently deflating it with your fingertips. Divide the dough into 16 pieces of the same size and then roll them into round balls.

3. With a cooking spray, spray a 13*9 inches pan and place the dough balls on the pan, positioning them right next to each other. Using a cloth towel, cover the pan and leave it to rest for 60 minutes. The rolls would practically double in size

throughout this period.

4. Preheat the oven to 350°F. Bake them in the oven for 16-18 minutes or until the surface of the rolls is golden brown. Remove from the oven and allow them to cool down.

5. Serve warm.

6.5 Buttery (Whole Wheat) Bread Machine Rolls

Total time

2 hours 20 minutes

Servings

18 servings

Nutrition facts

170 calories per serving

Ingredients

Here is the list of ingredients required to make buttery buns.

- 1 cup all-purpose flour

- 1 cup lukewarm milk

- 3 cups whole wheat flour

- ½ cup butter at room temperature

- 2 eggs

- ¼ cup sugar

- ¾ tsp. salt

- 3 tsp. instant yeast

- ¼ to ½ additional water or milk

Method

Follow the instructions below to make buttery (whole wheat rolls)

1. Place all the mentioned ingredients in your bread machine (in the order given). Start the cycle of dough. Keep on checking the dough in between the cycle to verify if it needs more flour or water. If the dough does not appear to be coming together properly, add an extra ¼ to ½ cup of milk or water.

2. Remove from the pan after the cycle has ended.

3. Shape into balls with pieces of dough and put in a greased bowl, leaving about an inch in between. (See above photos)

4. Cover and let the rolls expand until they double (about 30-45 minutes).

5. Preheat your oven to 350°F. Bake the rolls for about 20 minutes or until slightly golden brown.

6. Remove from the oven and slightly cool.

7. Serve at room temperature or warm.

6.6 Oatmeal Rolls with Honey

Total time

2 hours 45 minutes

Servings

14 servings

Nutrition facts

164 calories per serving

Ingredients

Here is the list of ingredients required to make oatmeal rolls with honey in a bread machine.

- 2 ½ cups bread flour

- 1 cup lukewarm milk

- 1 large egg

- ¼ cup unsalted butter

- q/4 cup honey

- ½ cup oats

- 1 tsp. salt

- 2 ¼ tsp. bread machine yeast

- 1 tbsp. wheat gluten

- 1 tbsp. water

- 1 egg

Method

Follow the instructions below to make Oatmeal rolls.

1. In the order mentioned, add all of the dough ingredients into the bread machine pan.

2. Select the dough cycle of the machine and push the start button.

3. Turn the dough out onto a floured surface as the dough cycle ends. Divide the dough equally into two parts. For a total of 14, split each half into 7 rolls. To turn each part into a smooth ball, use your fingers.

4. Place the balls of dough on a greased baking sheet. Let it rise to nearly double.

5. Switch on the oven for about 15 minutes until you expect the rolls to be ready for baking. Gently press down the rolls 1-3 times in the middle using the dull side of a thin knife or a wooden skewer.

6. Whisk together the eggs and water for the glaze and softly cover the rolls.

7. Bake for 10-13 minutes at 350. Let the rolls cool down for a few minutes before eating, so they do not burn your fingers.

8. Serve warm.

6.7 Bread Machine Mini Buns

Total time

55 minutes

Servings

10 servings

Nutrition facts

185calories per serving

Ingredients

Here is the list of ingredients required to make bread machine mini buns.

- 1 cup milk

- 2 tbsp. melted butter

- 1 tsp. salt

- 2 ½ tsp active dry yeast

- 3 ¼ cups all-purpose flour

- 1 large egg

- 3 tbsp. sugar

Method

Follow the instructions below to make mini buns.

1. Collect the ingredients.

2. Whisk together the milk, egg, and melted butter in a bowl or big cup. Put the milk mixture, sugar, flour, 1 tsp. of salt, and yeast in the bread machine. Run-on the cycle of dough.

3. On a lightly floured board, scrape the finished dough. Roll half of the dough to a thickness of around 1/4-inch to 1/3-inch. Depending on the size you like, cut it out

with a 1 1/2- to a 3-inch cutter. With the leftover dough, repeat the same steps.

4. Place them about 2 to 3 inches apart on a thinly greased baking sheet. Cover and let rise until doubled in size, about 30 minutes.

5. Your oven should be preheated to 350 °F

6. Bake the buns for almost15 18 minutes, or until they are browned properly. Brush the tops when they're hot with a little butter. On a cooling rack, let them cool.

7. Cut the cooled buns from the center and use them as required for sliders or filling.

8. Enjoy.

6.8 Bread Machine Cinnamon buns

Total time

4 hours 35 minutes

Servings

12 servings

Nutrition facts

224 calories per serving

Ingredients

Here is the list of ingredients required to make cinnamon buns.

- 3 ½ cup bread flour

- ¼ cup butter(softened)

- 3 tbsp. sugar

- 1 large egg

- ½ tsp. salt

- 1 cup milk

- 2 tsp. active dry yeast

- ¼ cup butter (melted)

- ¼ cup sugar

- ½ cup nuts

- 2 tsp. cinnamon powder

- ½ tsp. nutmeg

- 1 to 2 tbsp. milk or cream

- 1 cup icing sugar

- ½ tsp. vanilla extract

Method

Follow the instructions below to make cinnamon buns.

1. Collect the ingredients.

2. As suggested by the maker, add milk, butter, flour, sugar, yeast, egg, and salt to your bread machine for the dough. For the dough cycle, set the appliance. Let the dough knead.

3. Place the formed dough on a floured surface until the loop is finished. For about a minute, knead the dough, then let it rest for a further 15 minutes.

4. Roll out the dough, about 15 by 10 centimeters, into a rectangle shape.

5. Over the dough, brush the 1/4 cup melted butter to within 1 inch of the sides.

6. In a cup, add together the butter, cinnamon, chopped nuts, and nutmeg. Sprinkle generously over the dough with the mixture.

7. Roll the dough up firmly, starting on the long side. To seal and mold into 12-inch-long, uniformly rounded buns, press the sides.

8. Cut the whole roll into 1-inch bits with a knife or an 8-inch-long strip of uncoated dental floss.

9. Grease a baking pan that is 13 x 9 inches.

10. Place the cut-side of buns facing the pan. Cover and let rise until they double in size in a warm point. This will take 30 to 45 minutes or so.

11. Preheat your oven to 375 °F.

12. For almost 20 to 25 minutes or until golden brown, bake the buns.

13. In a cup, combine the milk, vanilla, and powdered sugar. Blend the mixture until smooth. Add more powdered sugar or milk whether it is too thin or too thick before the perfect consistency is met.

14. Cool the buns for 10 to 15 minutes in the pan. Once they are covered with sauce sprinkle some icing sugar on them.

15. Your cinnamon buns are ready to serve.

6.9 Sweet Potato Sandwich Rolls

Total time

2 hours 27 minutes

Servings

9 servings

Nutrition facts

135 calories per serving

Ingredients

Here is the list of ingredients required to make sweet potato sandwich rolls.

- 3 cups all-purpose flour

- 2 tbsp. sugar

- 1 sweet potato (medium-sized)

- 2 ¼ tsp. instant yeast

- 1 tsp. salt

- 1 large egg

- ½ cup milk

- 3 tbsp. butter (softened)

- 1 tbsp. water

- 1 large egg white

- Poppy seeds or sesame seeds

Method

Follow the instructions below to make sweet potato sandwich rolls

1. Collect the ingredients.

2. The sweet potato should be peeled and cut into cubes. Place it in a soup pot and cover it with water. On high heat, bring the water to a boil; reduce the heat to medium-low, cover the pan and continue cooking until the sweet potato is tender. Thoroughly drain the potato chunks and then mash them until smooth. Measure 3/4 of a cup of the puree and set it to cool aside.

3. Combine 2 1/2 cups of the flour with the salt, yeast, and sugar in a large size mixing bowl.

4. Whisk the milk with the egg, the cooled sweet potatoes, and the softened butter in a separate dish.

5. To the dry ingredients, add the sweet potato mixture and combine until moistened.

6. Attach the dough hook and continue to knead the dough for 8 minutes, as needed, adding more than the remaining 1/2 cup of flour. The dough's going to be a bit sticky.

7. In a wide buttered pan, form the dough into a ball and position it. Turn the dough until it is thoroughly coated with butter. Tightly cover the bowl with plastic wrap and let the dough rise in a warm place for approximately 1 hour, or until doubled.

8. Line the parchment paper on two baking sheets.

9. On a floured surface, remove the dough. The dough will weigh approximately 27 ounces. Cut into 9 (3-ounce) portions of the dough. Shape pieces of the dough into balls.

10. Take a ball of the dough formed and stretch it out on the work surface into a 12-inch rope.

11. Make an overhand knot with the rope which is also called a granny knot or single knot. Leave some space in the middle of the knot and the two long ends. Loop one end around the circle created by the knot (once or twice as it will depend on the length of ends). Use the other end to repeat. On the prepared baking sheet, place the roll.

12. Repeat the same process with the remaining dough balls.

13. Cover the rolls with kitchen towels loosely and let them rise for 30 minutes in a warm place.

14. Preheat your oven to 375 °F.

15. Whisk the white part of the egg with the water in a little bowl or cup.

16. Brush the egg wash mixture gently over the rolls and, if you want sprinkle with sesame or poppy seeds.

17. Place the rolls in the oven and bake until golden brown, or for 16 to 18 minutes.

Chapter 7: Pizza Dough Recipes

7.1 Basic Pizza Dough

Total time

1 hour 55 minutes

Servings

6 servings

Nutrition facts

536 calories per serving

Ingredients

Here is the list of ingredients required to make basic pizza dough in a bread machine.

- 1 cup all-purpose flour

- 1 cup whole wheat flour

- 1 tbsp. sugar

- 1 tsp. salt

- 1 tbsp. butter (softened)

- 1 tsp. yeast

- ½ cup + 2 tbsp. warm water

Method

Follow the instructions below to make basic pizza dough.

1. Add all the mentioned ingredients in the order recommended by the manufacturer of your bread machine. Make sure the water is warm enough for the yeast to rise.

2. Switch to the dough setting of your bread machine and let's go. Check the dough after a few minutes. Be sure to properly mix the ingredients and that the dough is not too moist or too dry. Add 1 tsp. of warm water at a time if it's too dry. Then add 1 tsp of flour at a time if the dough is too wet.

3. During the dough stage, the dough can rise well.

4. Load the dough out on a gently floured surface and work it until you reach the perfect form.

5. You will need the dough depending on the size of the pizza pan or pizza stone you are using.

6. Gently spray some oil and dust some cornmeal on your pizza pan Make the pizza and bake it for 18-25 minutes at 400-425 °F. Before baking, sprinkle some olive oil on the crust if you prefer a crunchier crust.

7.2 Bread Machine Thin Crust Pizza Dough

Total time

1 hour 15 minutes

Servings

8 servings

Nutrition facts

126 calories per serving

Ingredients

Here is the list of ingredients required to make a thin crust in pizza dough a bread machine.

- 2 cups all-purpose flour

- ¼ tsp. sugar

- 1 cup lukewarm water

- 1 tsp. active dry yeast

- ½ tsp. salt

- 2 tbsp. olive oil

Method

Follow the instructions below to make thin-crust pizza dough.

1. Pour the lukewarm water into the bread maker's pan and put the flour on top of the water. Sprinkle salt, sugar and add the yeast on top of the mixture.

2. Set the machine to the setting for the dough and press the start button.

3. Transfer to a well-floured work surface as the bread machine indicates that the dough is kneaded.

4. Preheat your oven to 425°F

5. Roll the dough into a thin crust about 14 inches wide or spread it out. Keep the edge

of the dough thick. On a 14-inch pizza baking dish, put the dough and spray the dough with olive oil.

6. Bake in a preheated oven for 5 minutes.

7.3 Italian Pizza Crust in Bread Machine

Total time

1 hour 15 minutes

Servings

8 servings

Nutrition facts

163 calories per serving

Ingredients

Here is the list of ingredients required to make Italian pizza crust in a bread machine.

- 2 ½ tsp. active dry yeast

- 2 ½ cups whole wheat flour

- 1 tsp. white sugar

- 2 tbsp. olive oil

- 1 ½ tsp. dried oregano

- 1 ½ tsp. dried basil

- 1 tsp. salt

- 1 cup lukewarm water

Method

Follow the instructions below to make Italian pizza crust.

1. In the pan of a bread machine, mix yeast, sugar, and warm water. Let it stand for about 10 minutes so the yeast softens and starts to form a creamy mixture.

2. Over the yeast mixture add olive oil, basil, flour, oregano, and salt. Place the bread machine bowl in the machine.

3. Choose the Dough settings and press Start.

7.4 Homemade Bread Machine Beer and basil Pizza Dough

Total time

30 minutes

Servings

12 servings

Nutrition facts

79 calories per serving

Ingredients

Here is the list of ingredients required to make beer and basil pizza dough.

- 3 cups all-purpose flour

- 3 tbsp. olive oil

- 1 tbsp. sugar

- 1 cup beer

- 1 tsp. salt

- 1 ½ tsp. dried basil leaves

- 1 ½ tsp. active dry yeast

Method

Follow the instructions below to make beer and basil pizza dough.

1. Collect the ingredients.

2. Put all the mentioned ingredients in the pan of your bread machine.

3. Choose the dough cycle and start the machine.

4. Remove the dough and spread it out to fit your thinly greased pizza pan when the loop finishes.

5. Cover with a towel and leave to rise for around 20 minutes longer in a warm place.

6. Top with your choice of toppings, sauce, and cheese range.

7. Se the temperature of the oven to 425 °F

8. Bake for around 15 to 20 minutes. Baking time will depend on the thickness of the toppings and crust

9. For a 14- to a 16-inch pizza, two 10-inch pizzas, or two small 12-inch crust pizzas, this amount of dough will be enough.

7.5 Homemade Bread Machine Beer Pizza Dough

Total time

30 minutes

Servings

12 servings

Nutrition facts

79 calories per serving

Ingredients

Here is the list of ingredients required to make beer pizza dough.

- 3 cups all-purpose flour

- 3 tbsp. olive oil

- 1 tbsp. sugar

- 1 cup beer

- 1 tsp. salt

- 1 ½ tsp. active dry yeast

Method

Follow the instructions below to make beer pizza dough.

1. Collect the ingredients.

2. In the order suggested by your bread machine maker, place all ingredients in the bread machine pan.

3. Choose the dough cycle and start the machine.

4. Remove the dough and spread it out to fit your thinly greased pizza pan when the loop finishes.

5. Cover with a towel and leave to rise for around 20 minutes longer in a warm place.

6. Top with your choice of toppings, sauce, and cheese range.

7. Se the temperature of the oven to 425 °F

8. Bake for around 15 to 20 minutes. Baking time will depend on the thickness of the toppings and crust

9. For a 14- to a 16-inch pizza, two 10-inch pizzas, or two small 12-inch crust pizzas, this amount of dough will be enough.

Conclusion

Working with a bread machine is fun. The more you figure out and realize what you can create with it, the more you will enjoy using it and keep one for you around.

It can take some experimentation, though. And a perfect way to cut the learning curve or get ideas is to get the recommended recipes in this cookbook. Despite the experience and skill level of how many years you've been making recipes using a bread machine, opening a cookbook will expose new recipes to you and help improve things.

Printed in Great Britain
by Amazon

72882633R00086